This workbook belongs to

Copyright © 2020
All rights reserved. No part of this publication may be reproduced, distributed,
or transmitted in any form or by any means, including photocopying, recording,
or other electronic or mechanical methods, without the prior written permission
of the publisher, except in the case of brief quotations embodied in critical reviews
and certain other noncommercial uses permitted by copyright law.

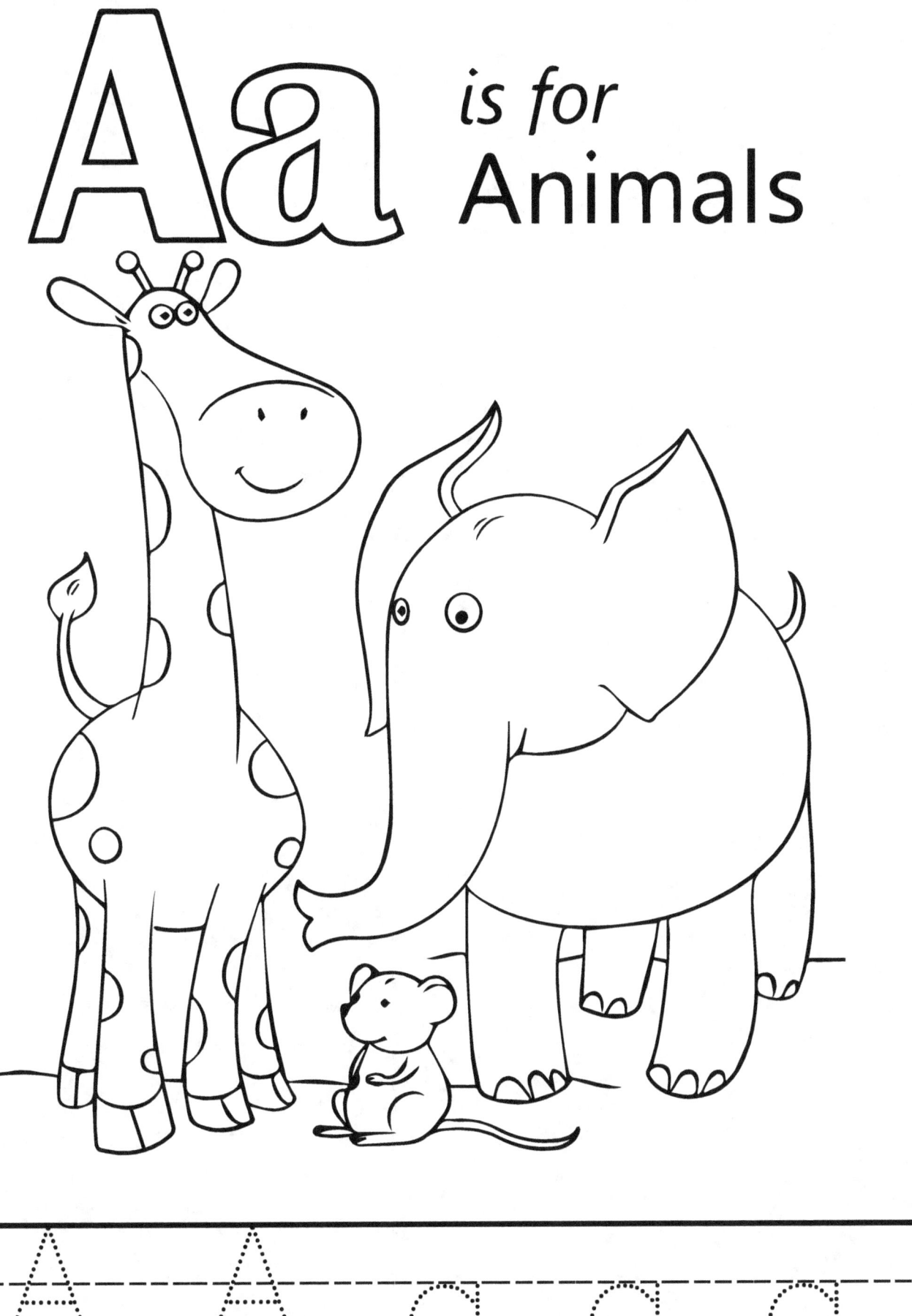

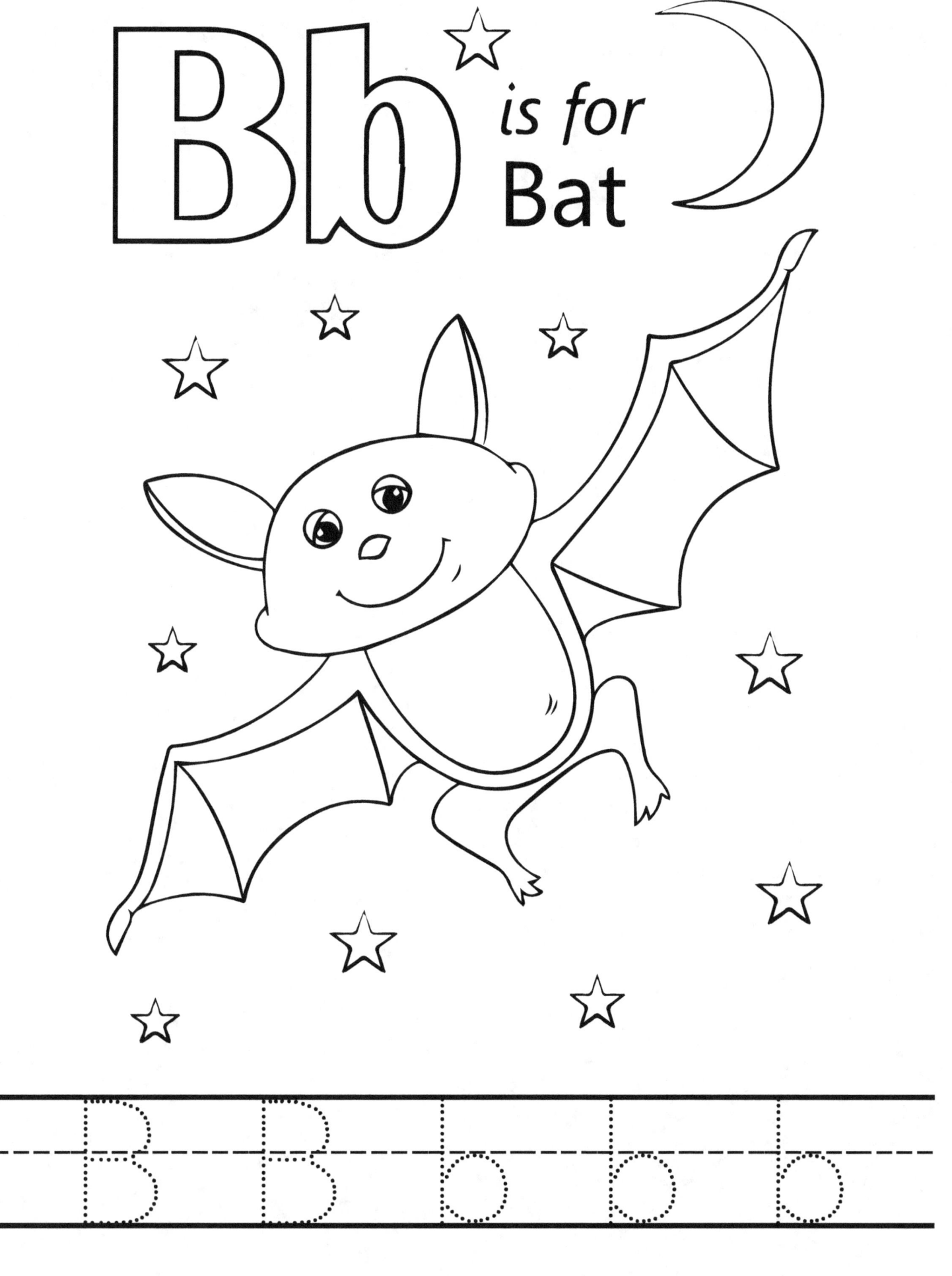

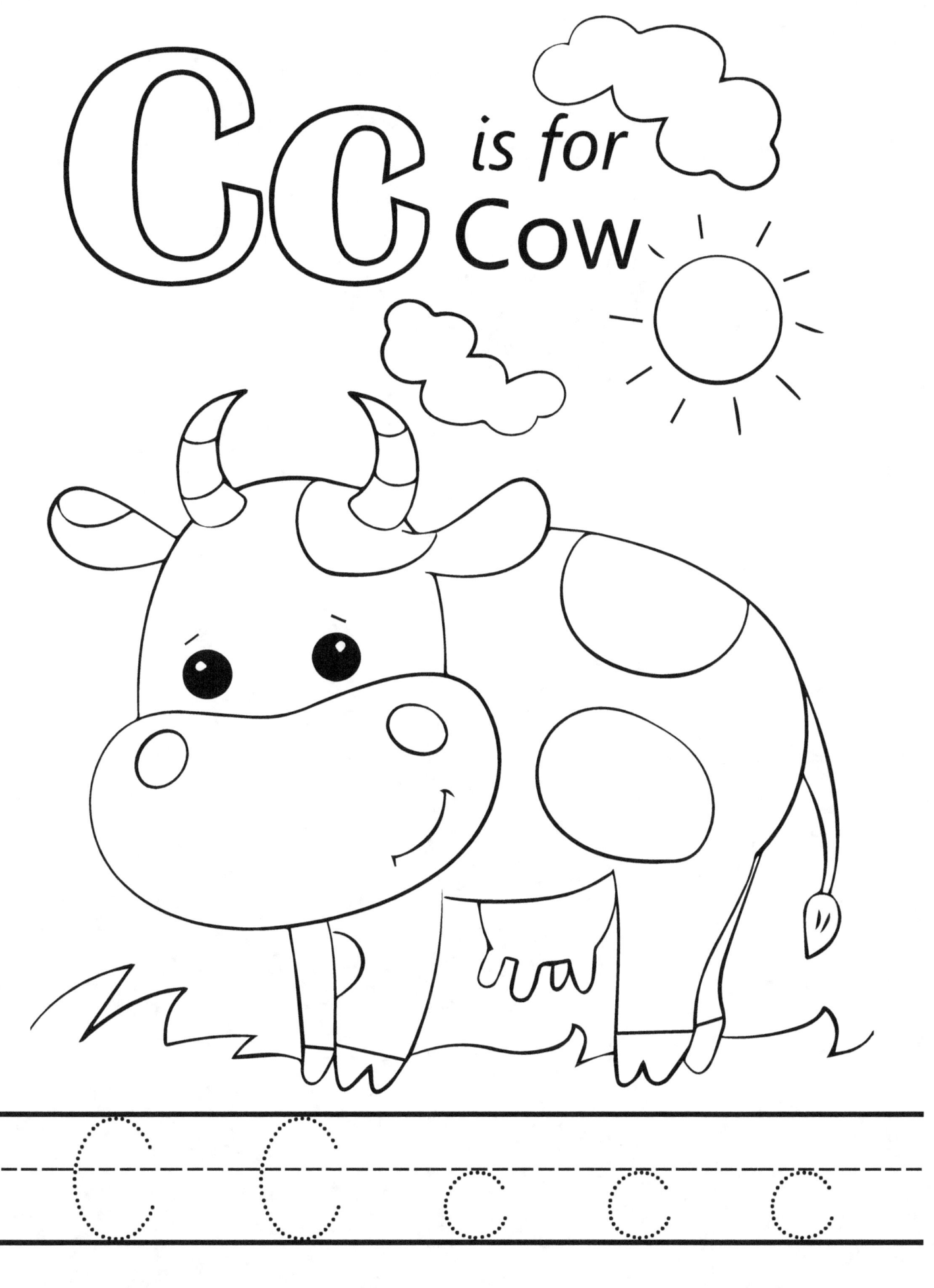

Dd is for Dolphin

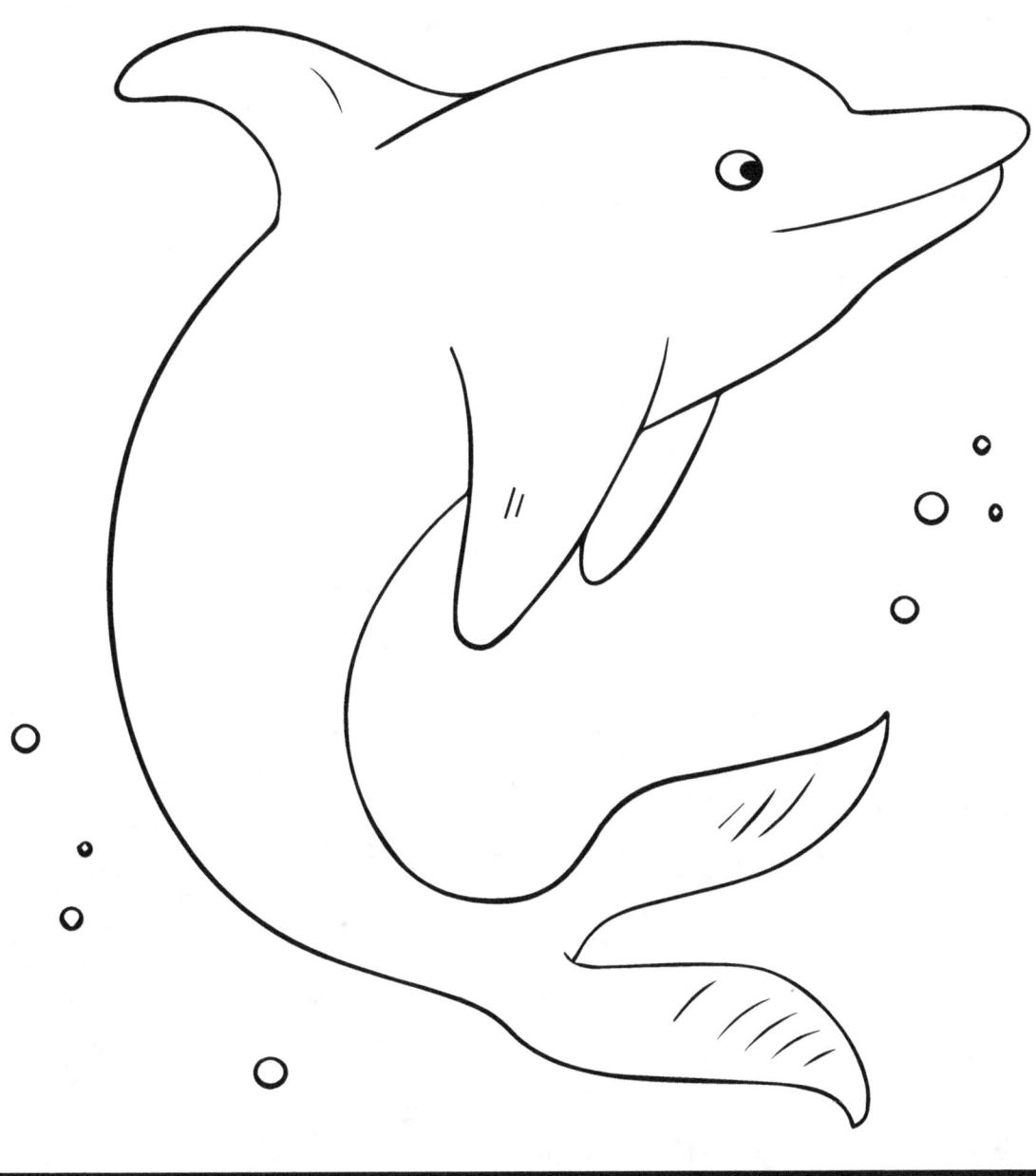

D D d d d

Ee is for Egg

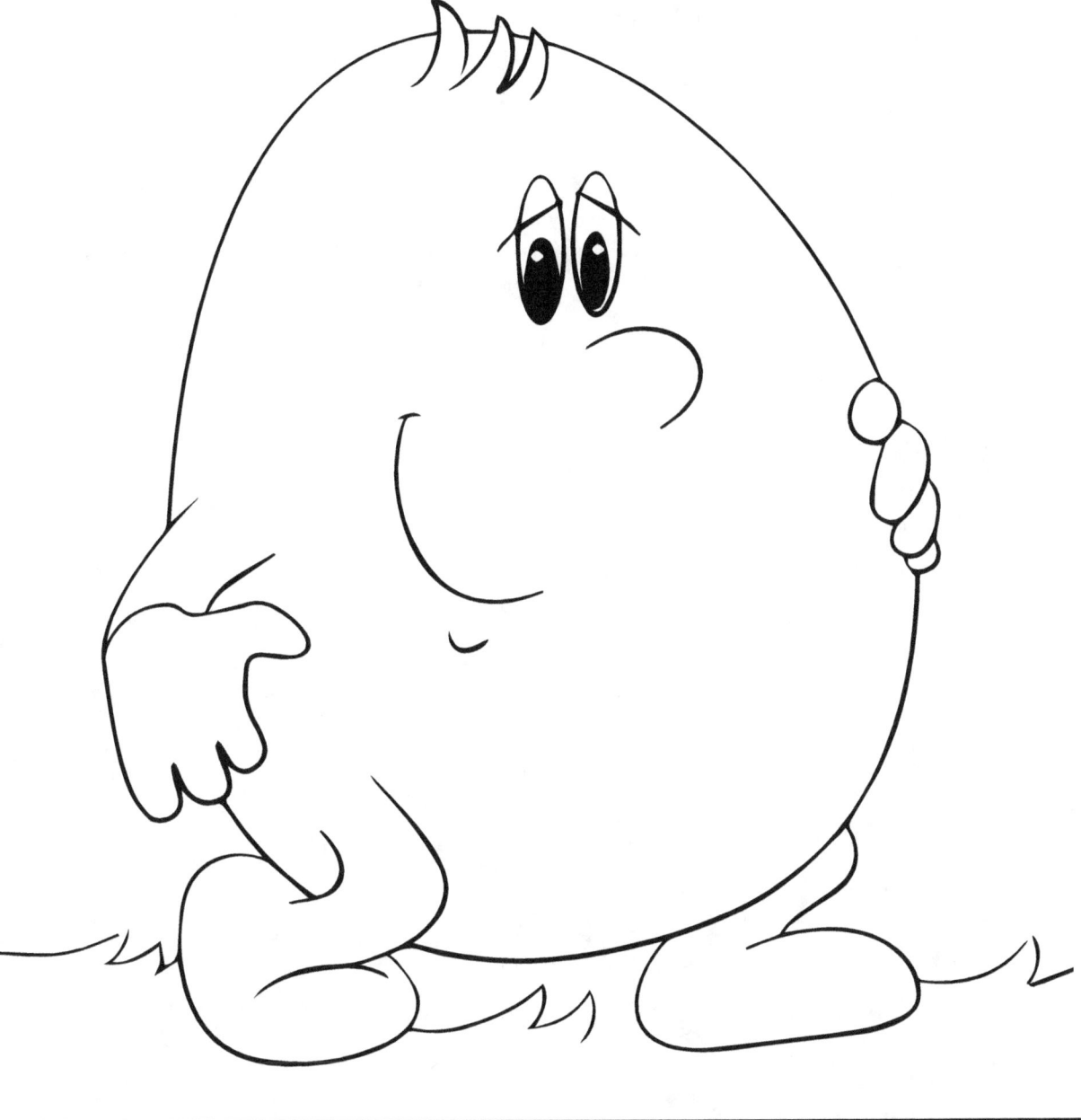

E e e e e

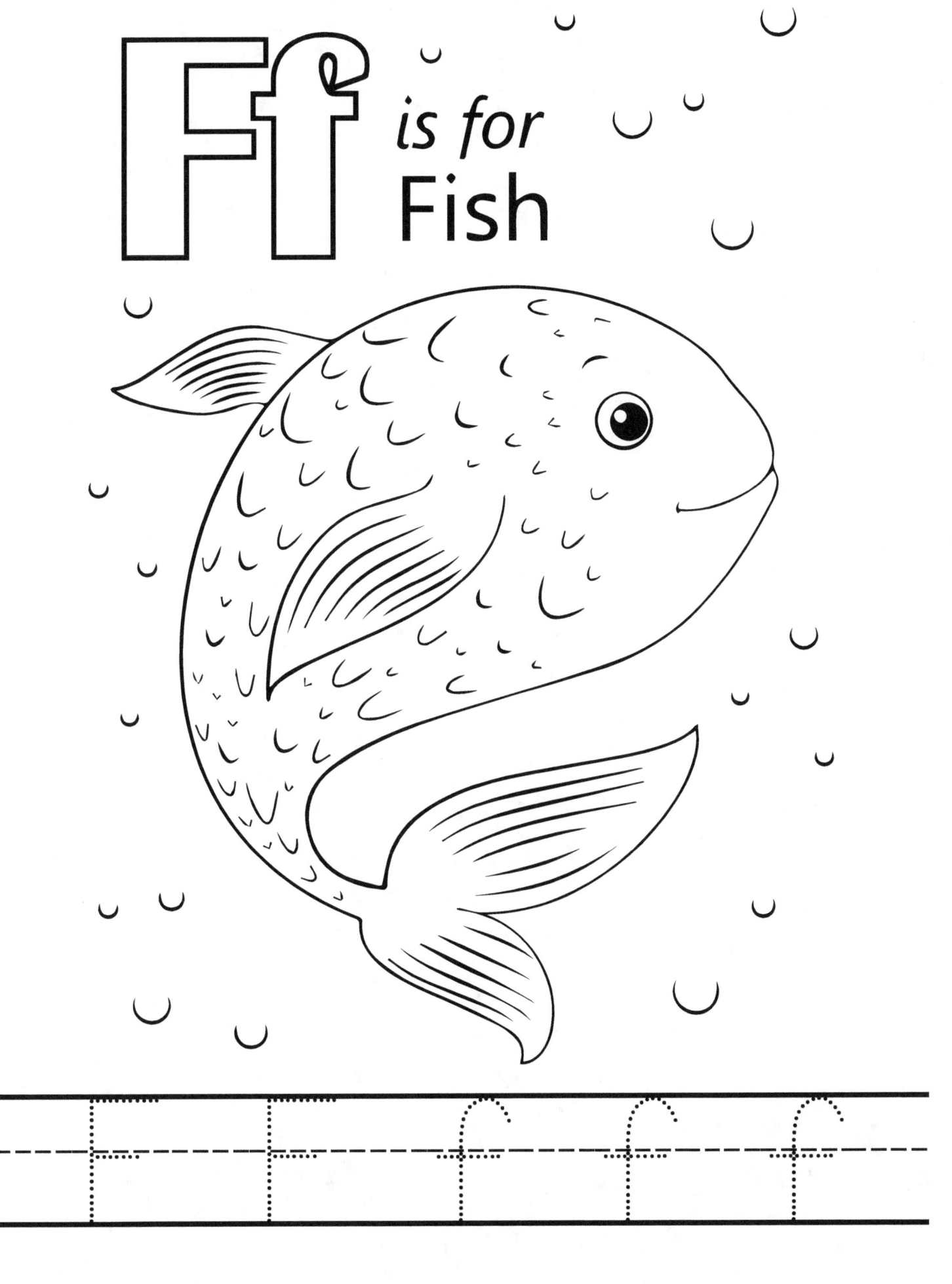

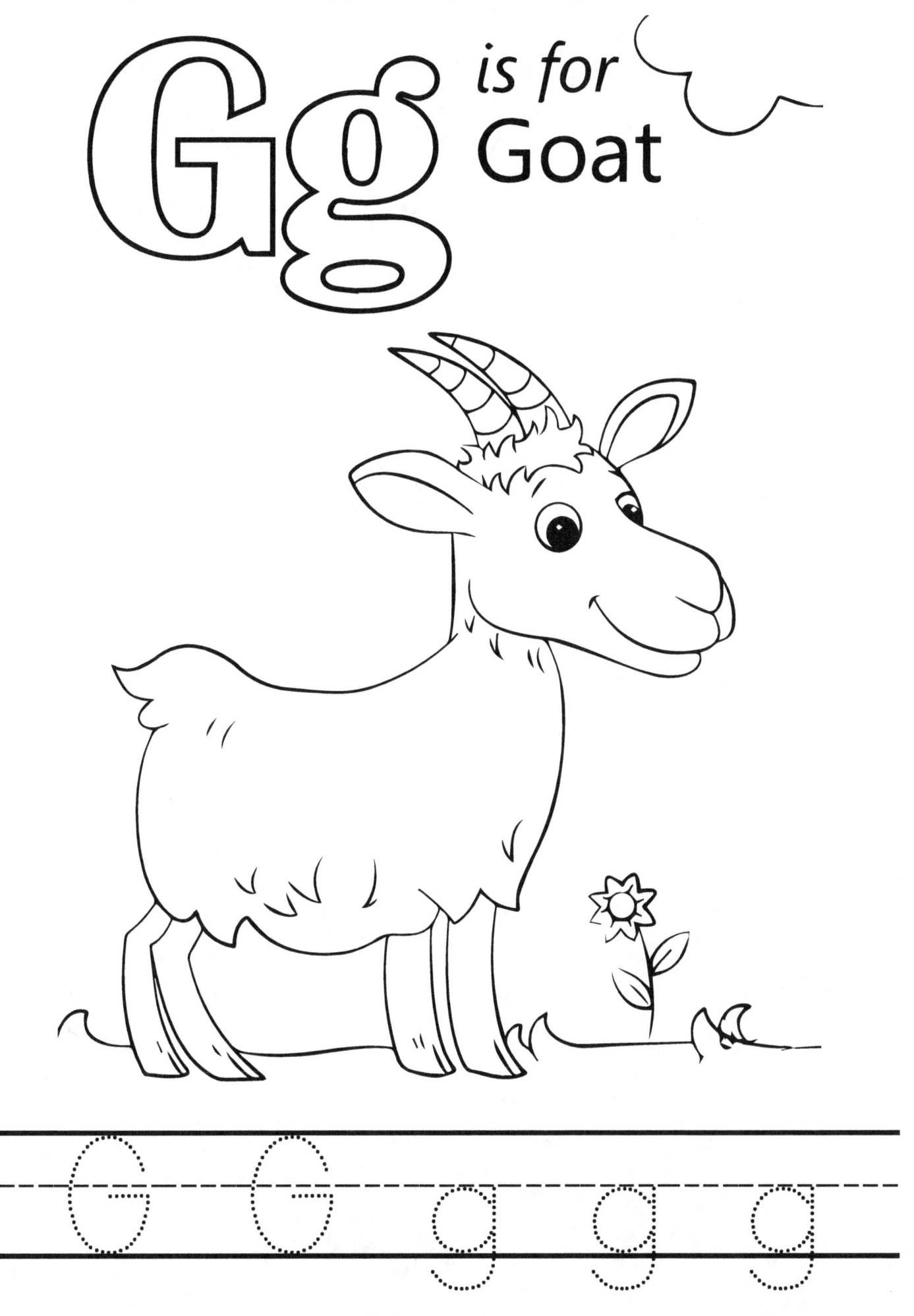

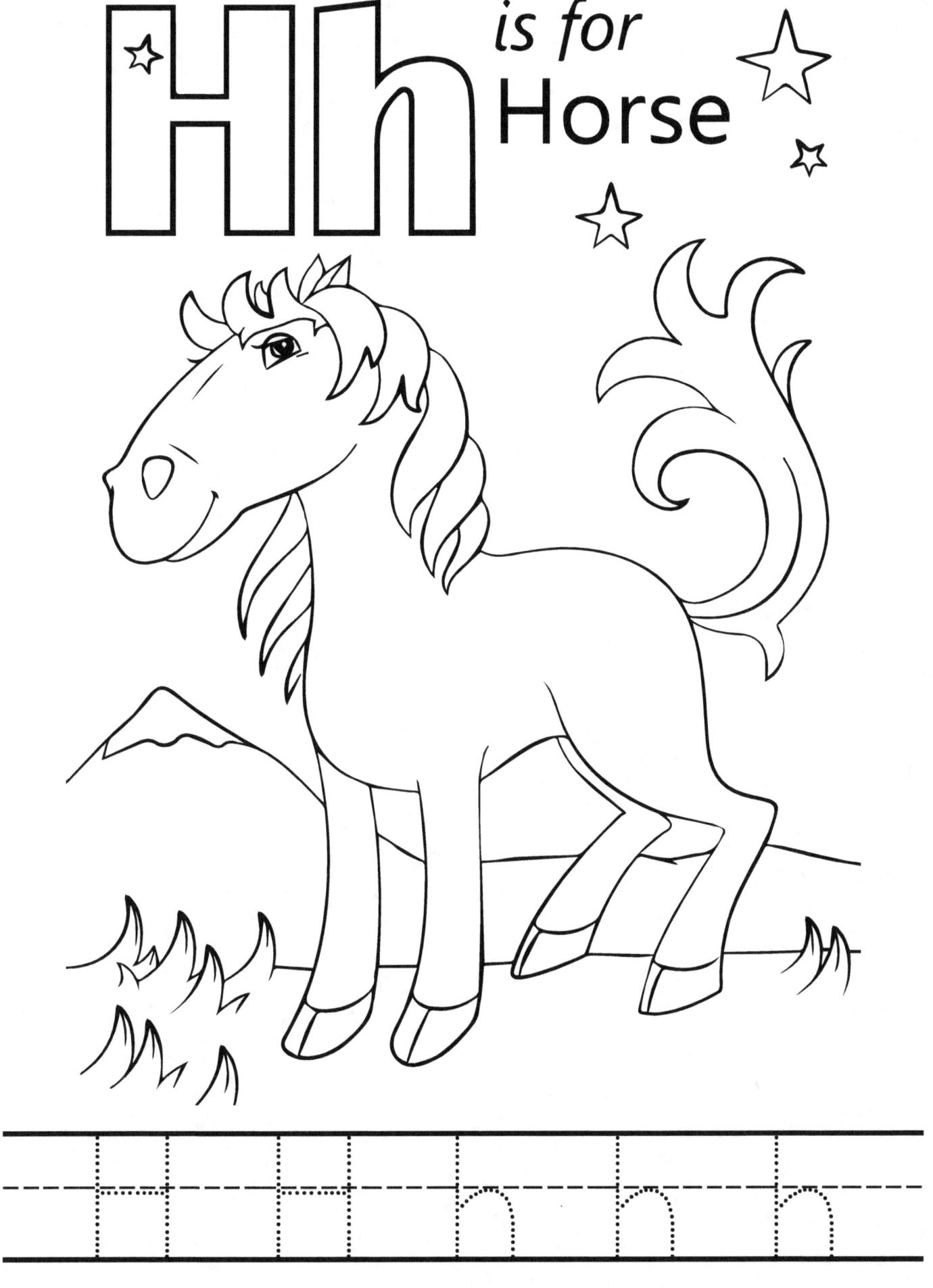

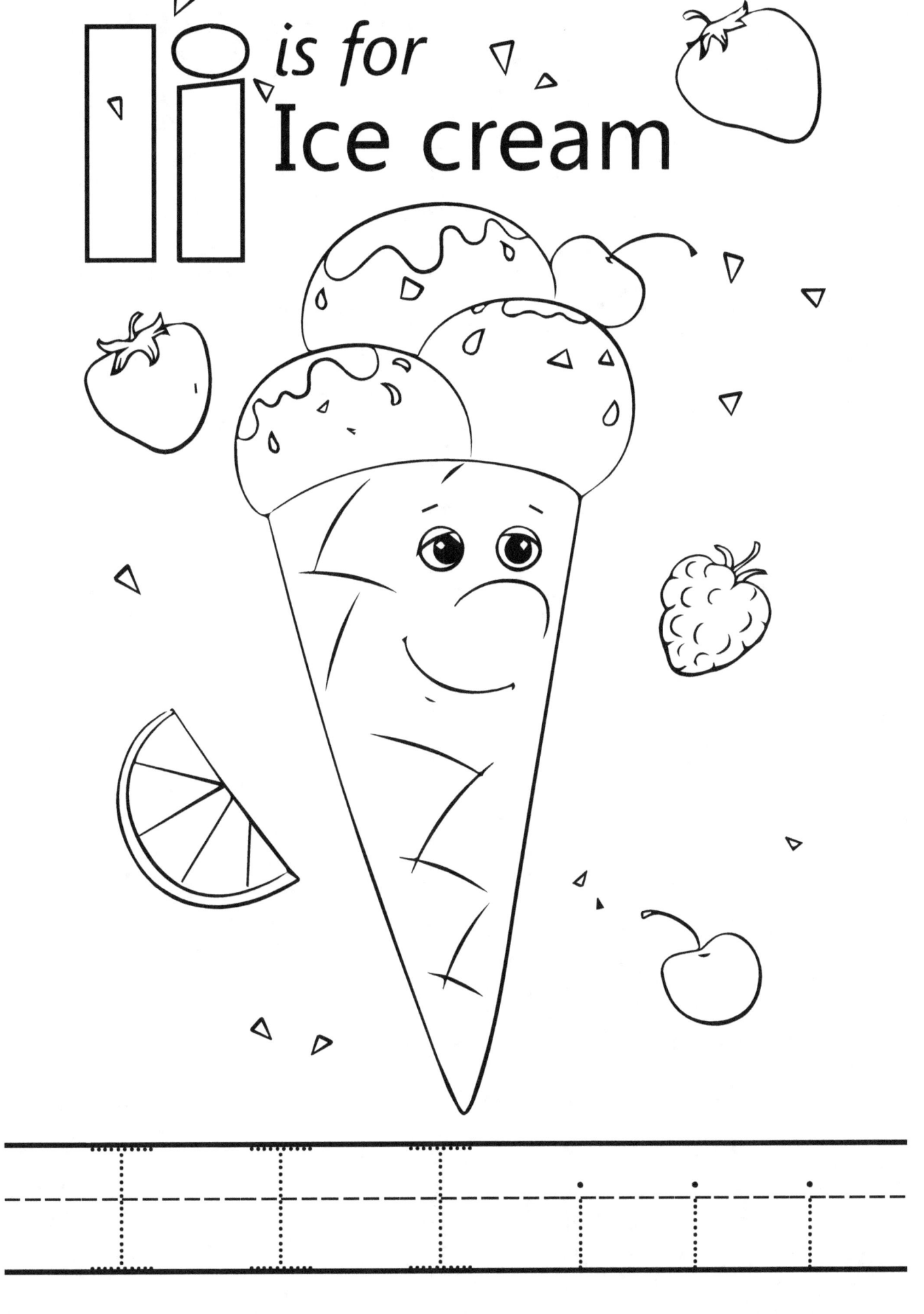

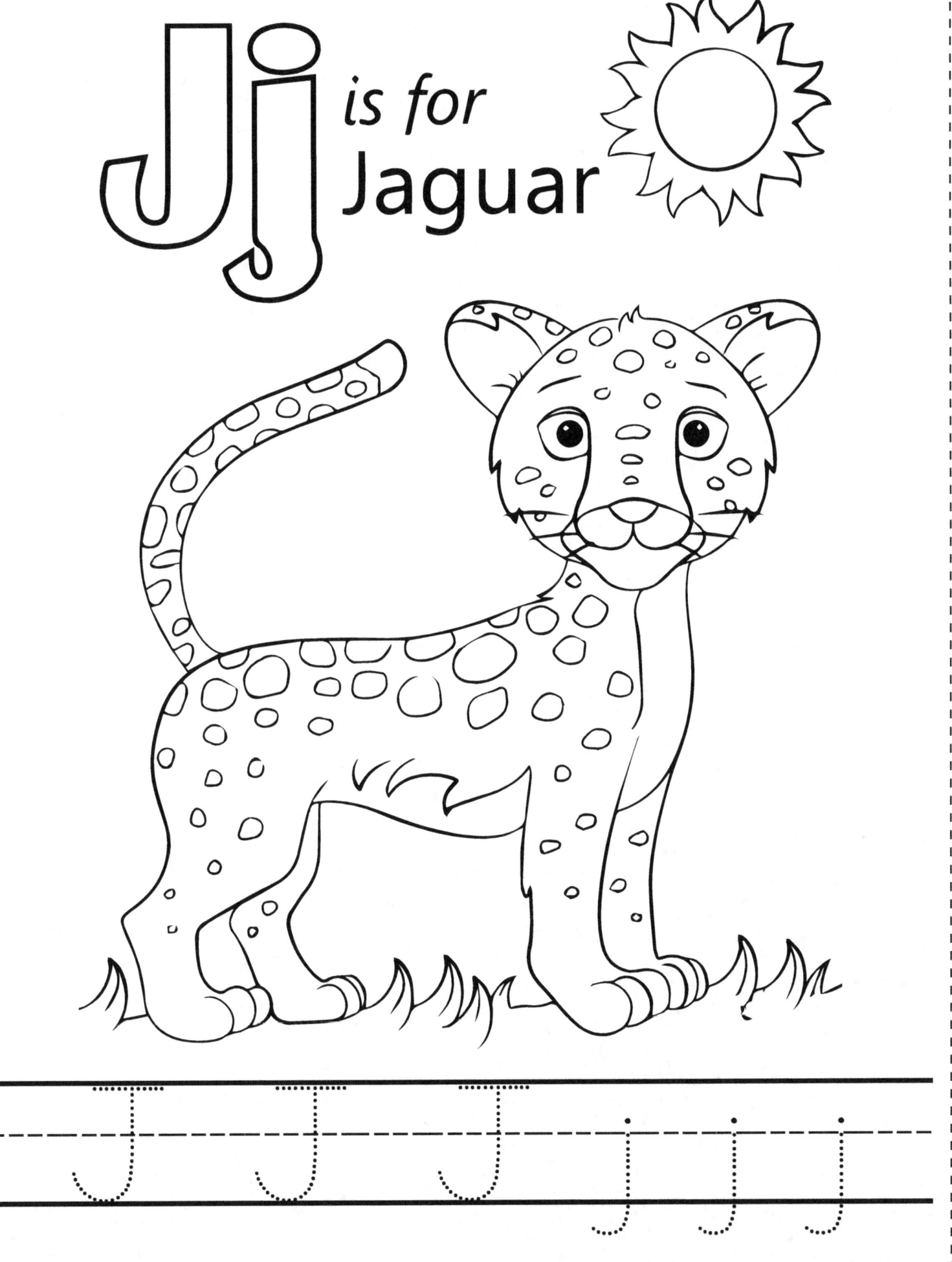

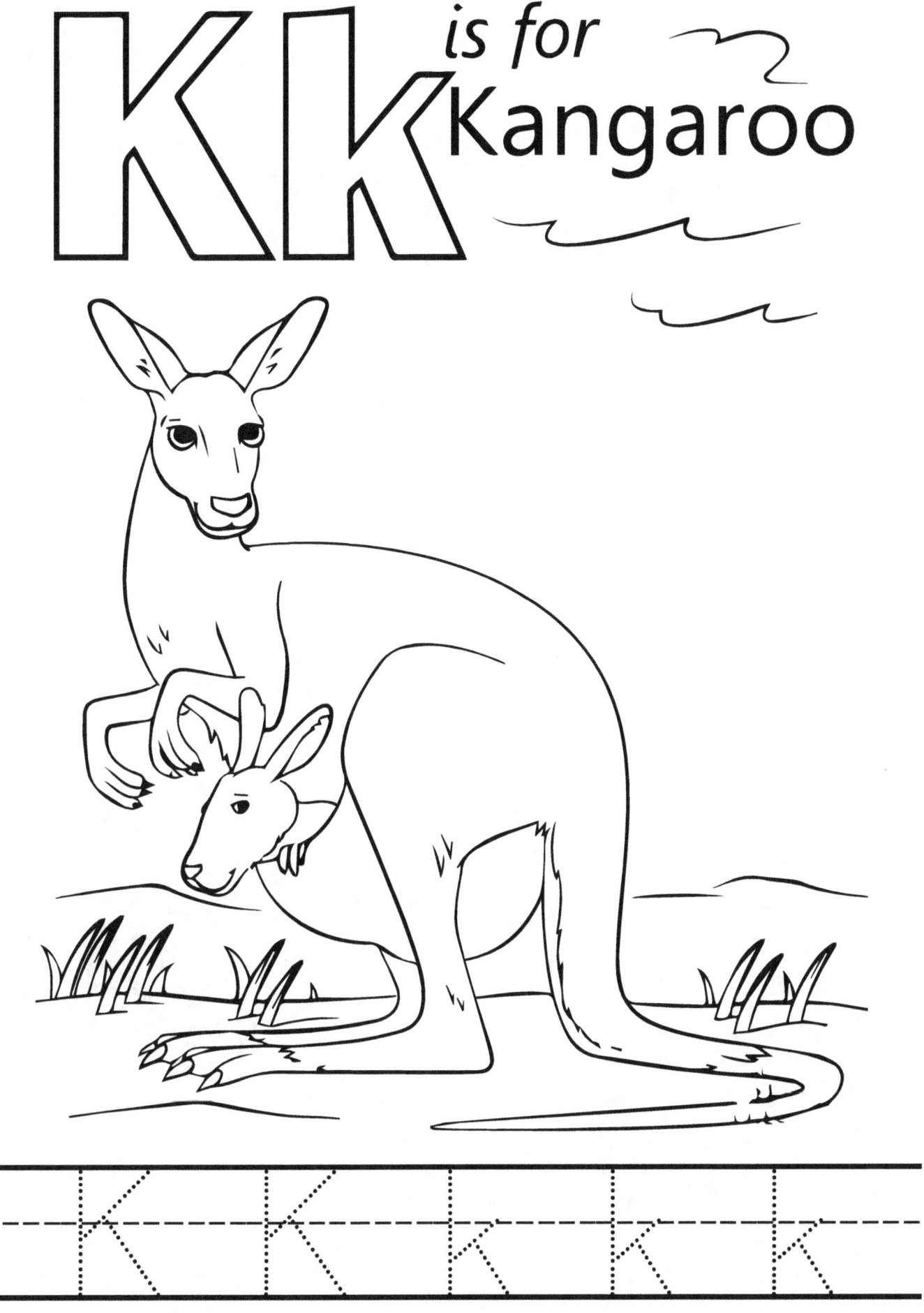

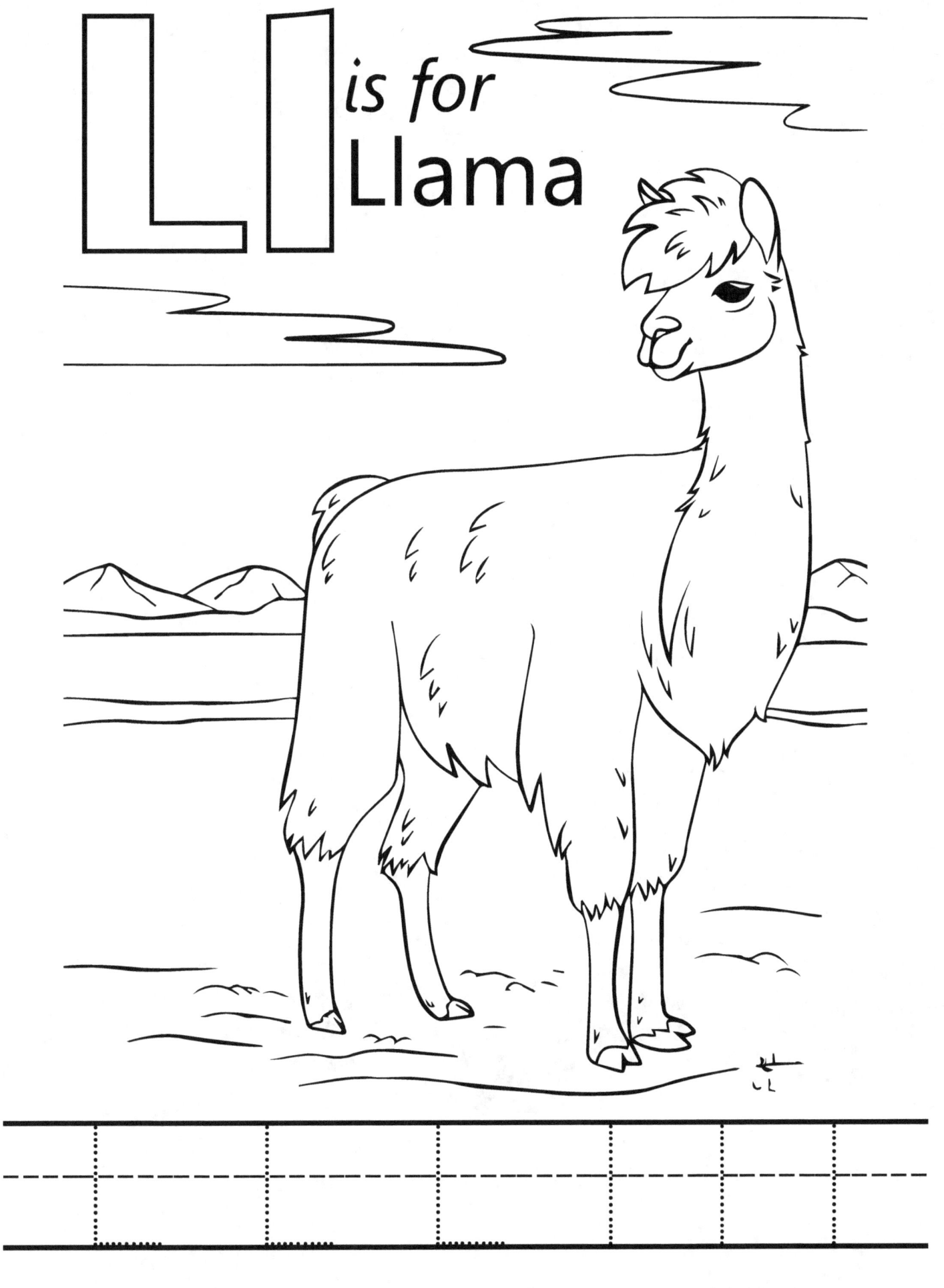

Mm is for Mouse

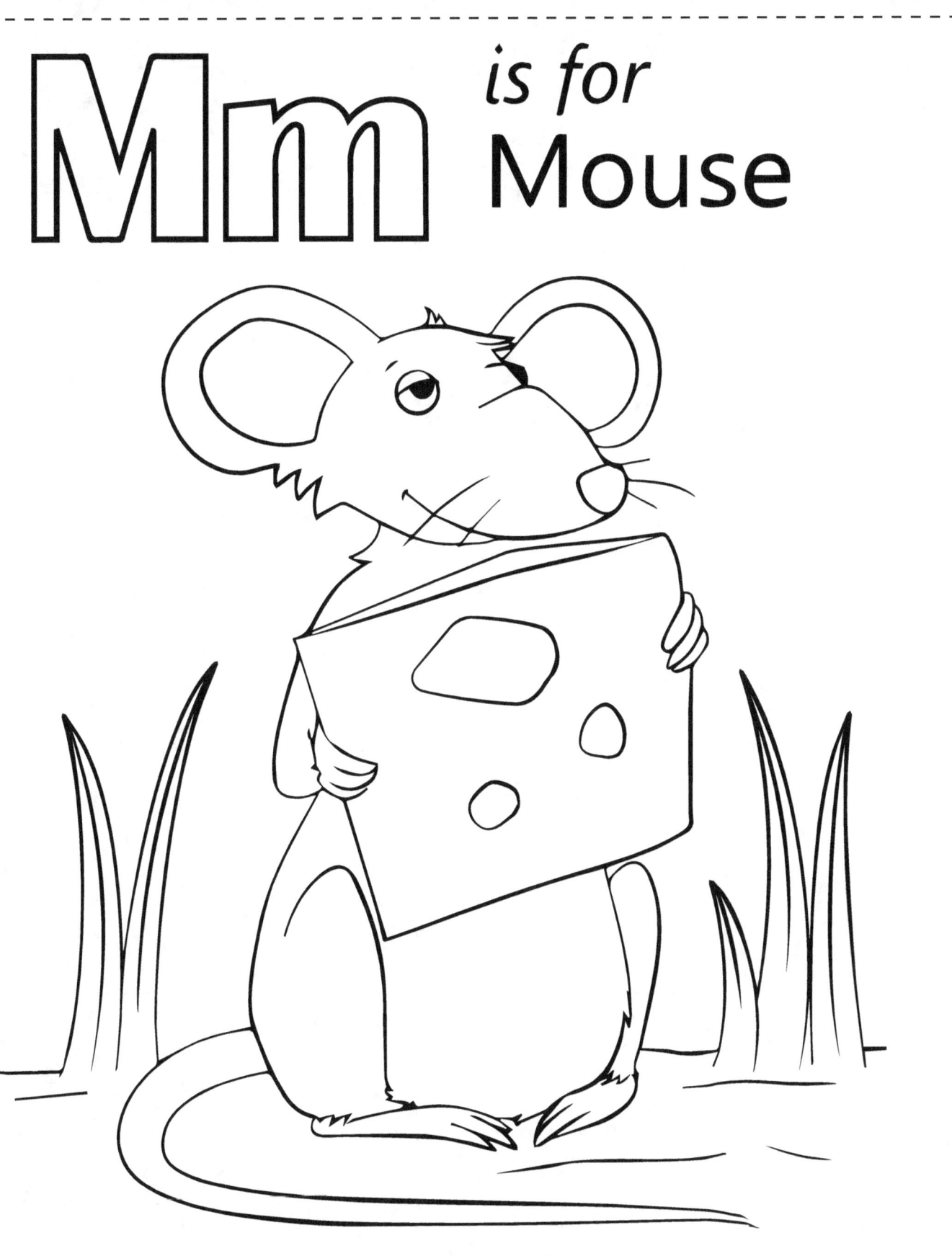

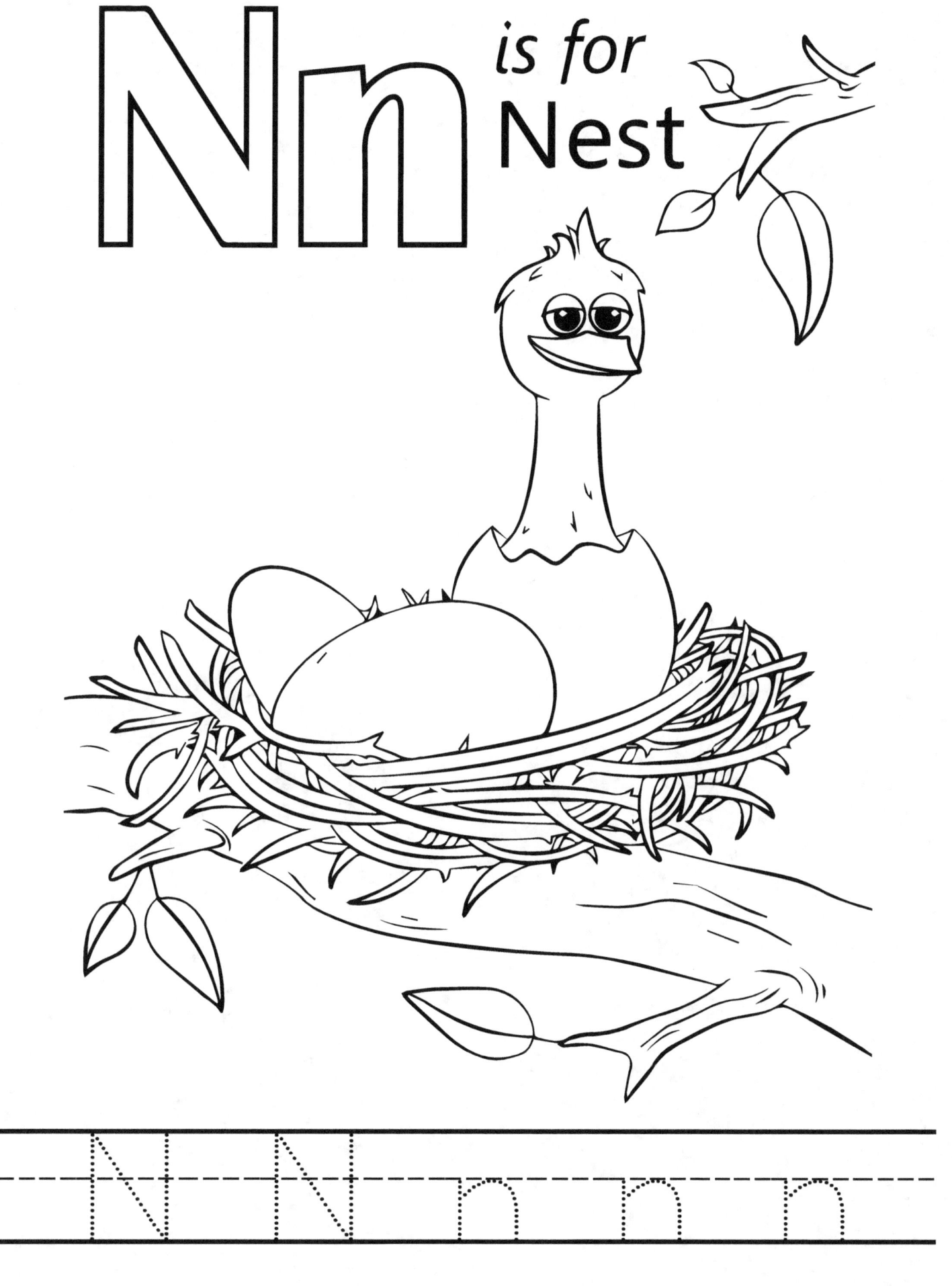

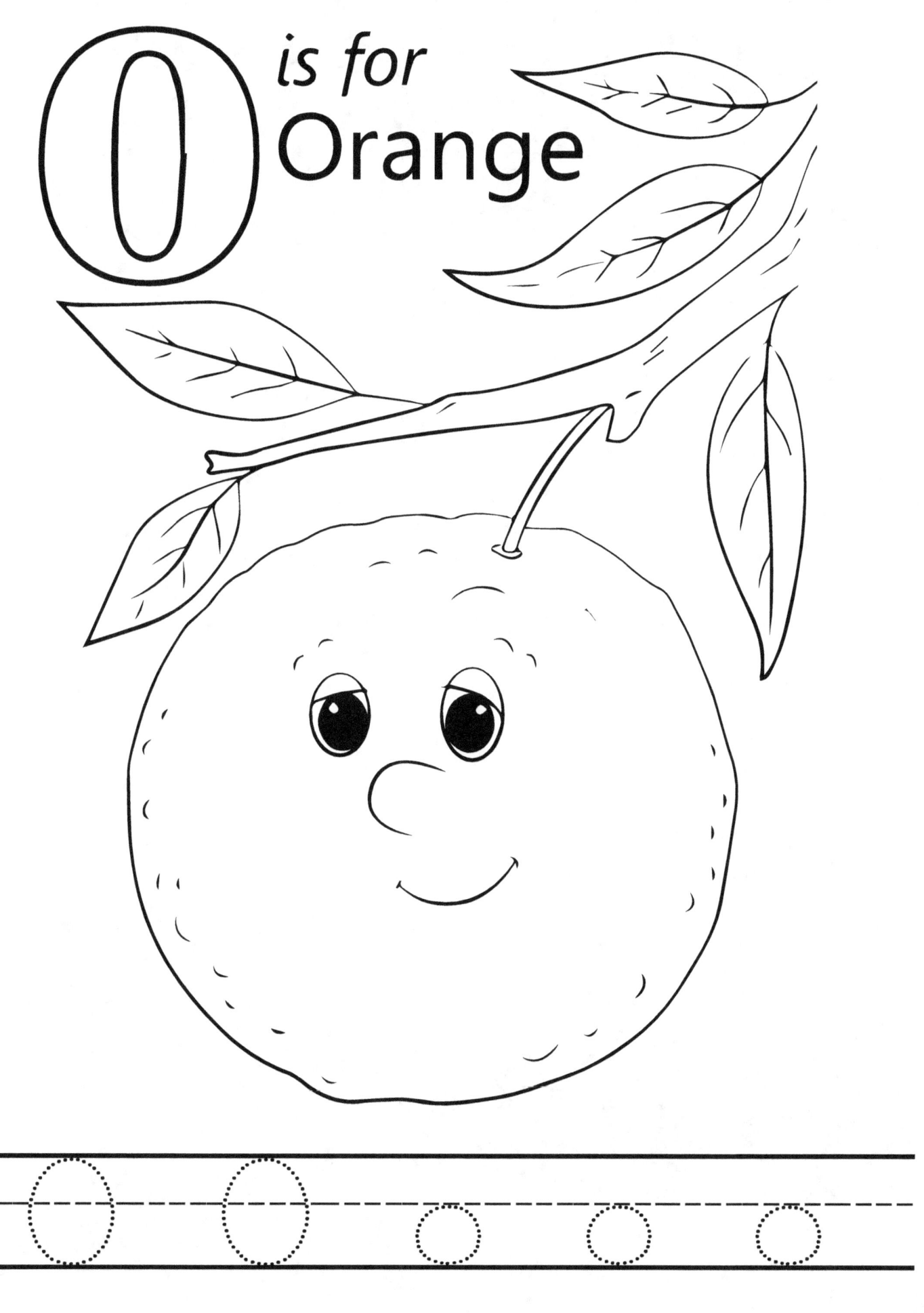

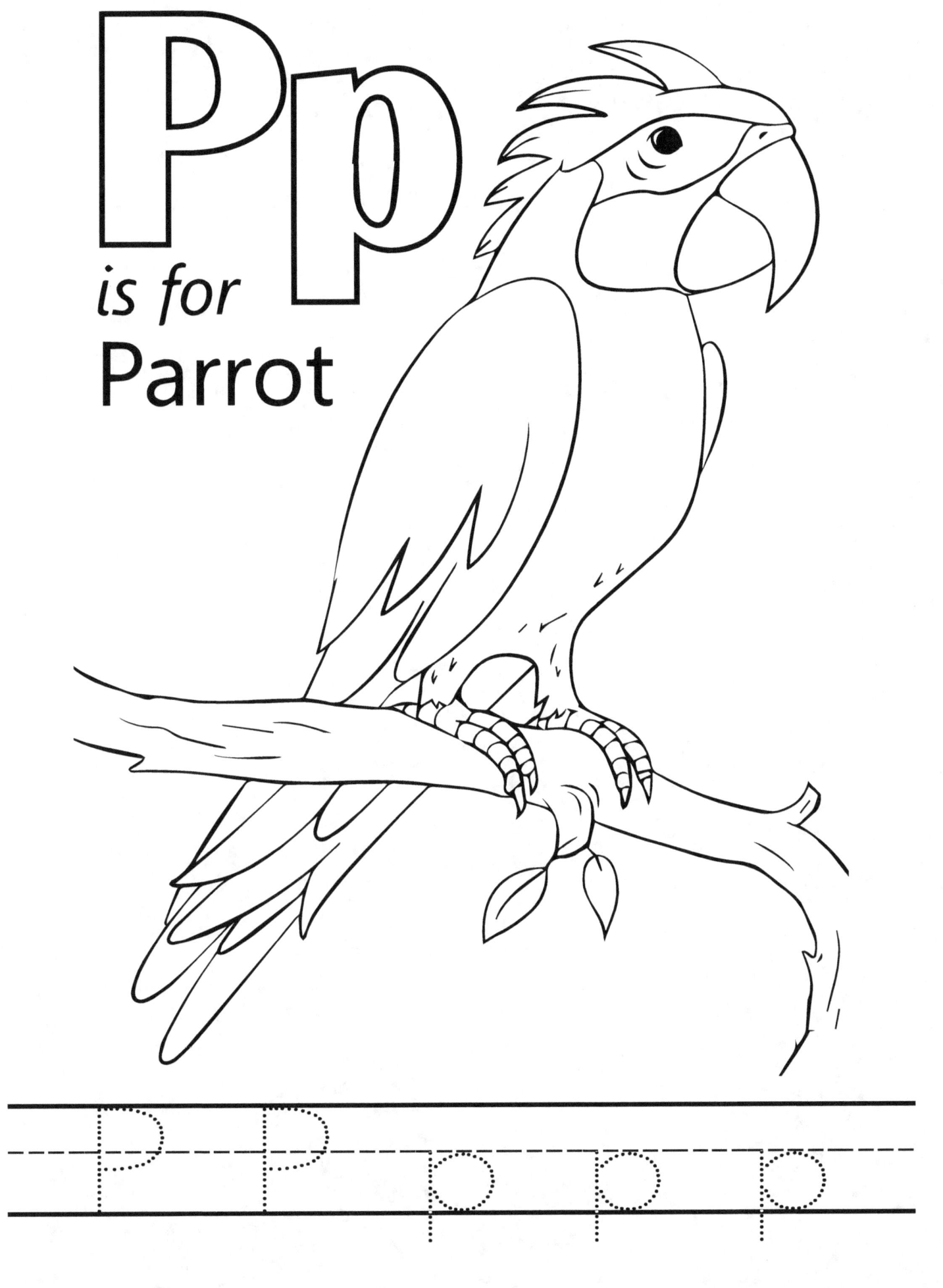

Q q *is for* Quail

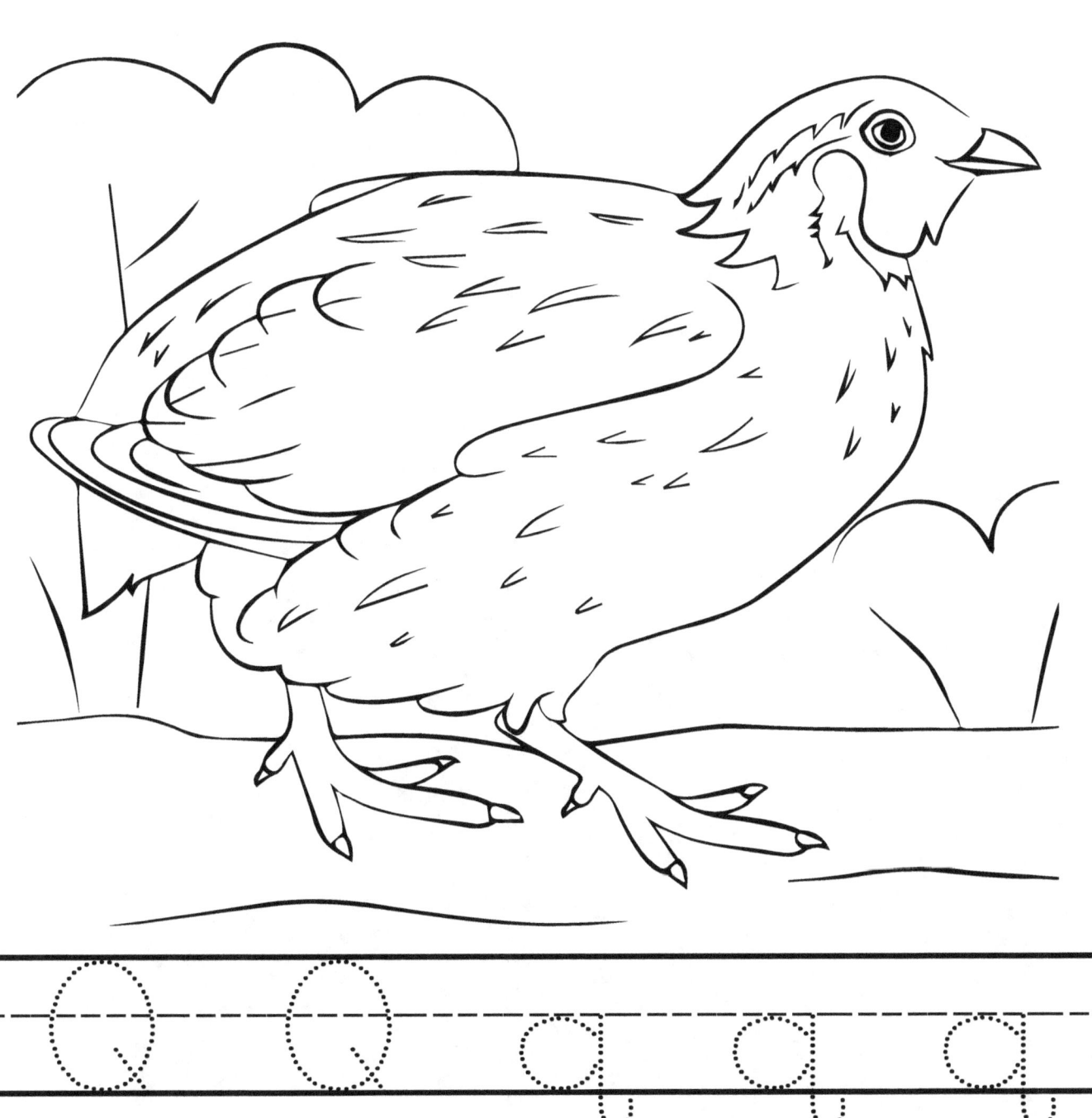

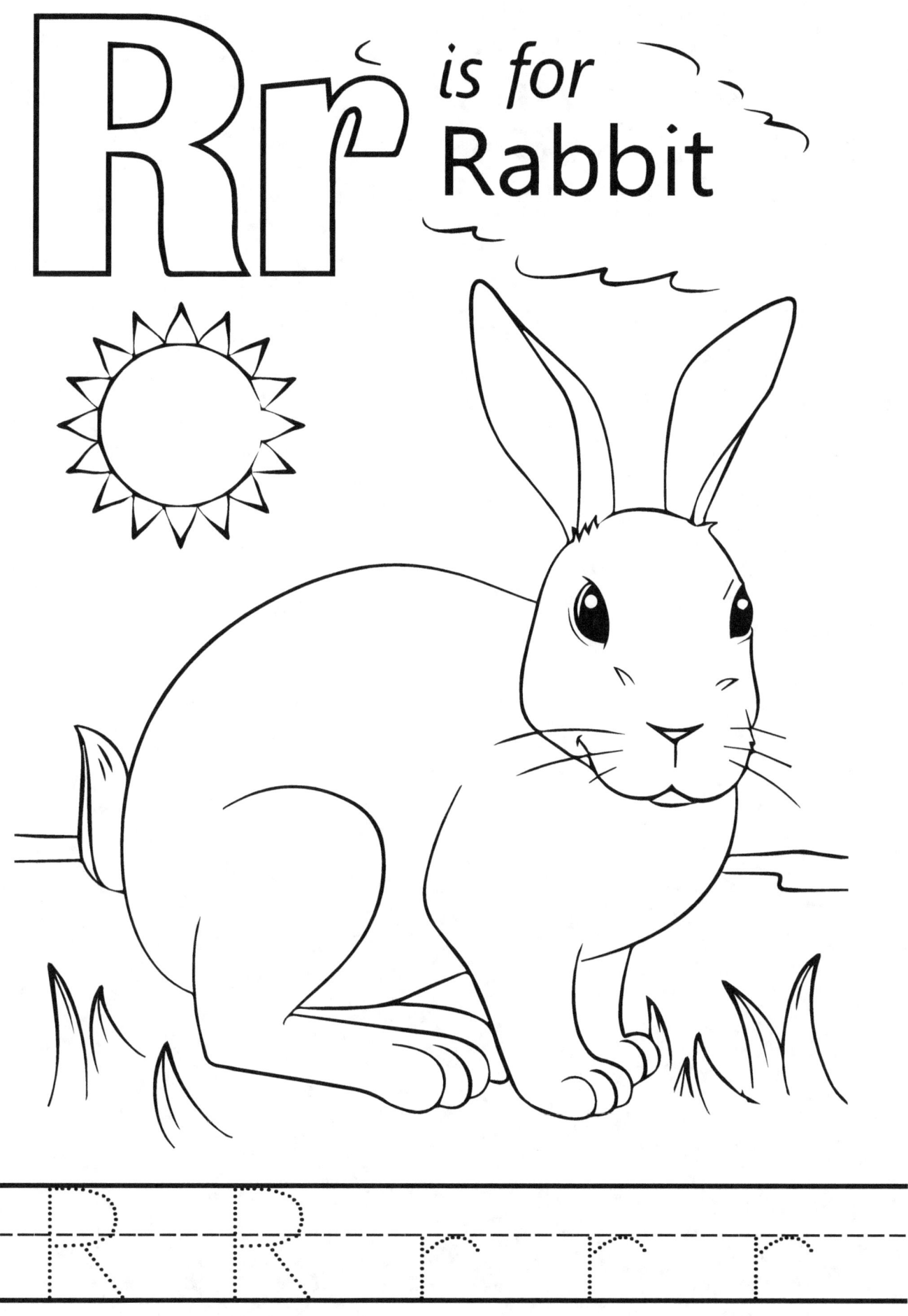

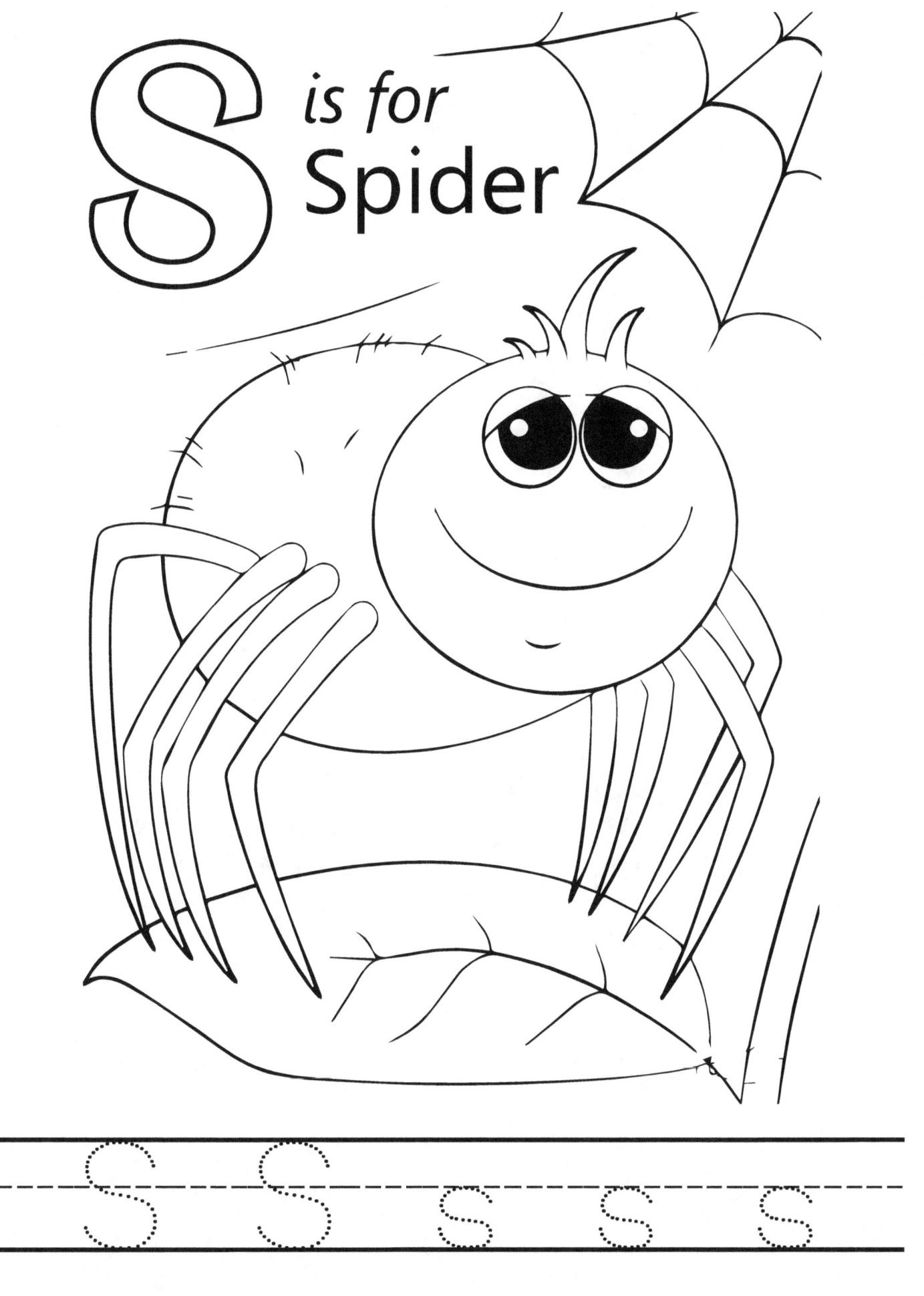

Tt is for Turtle

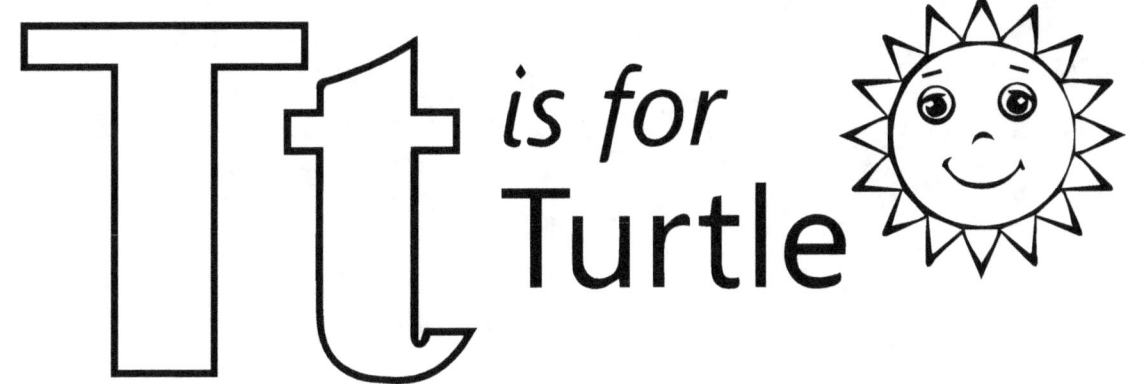

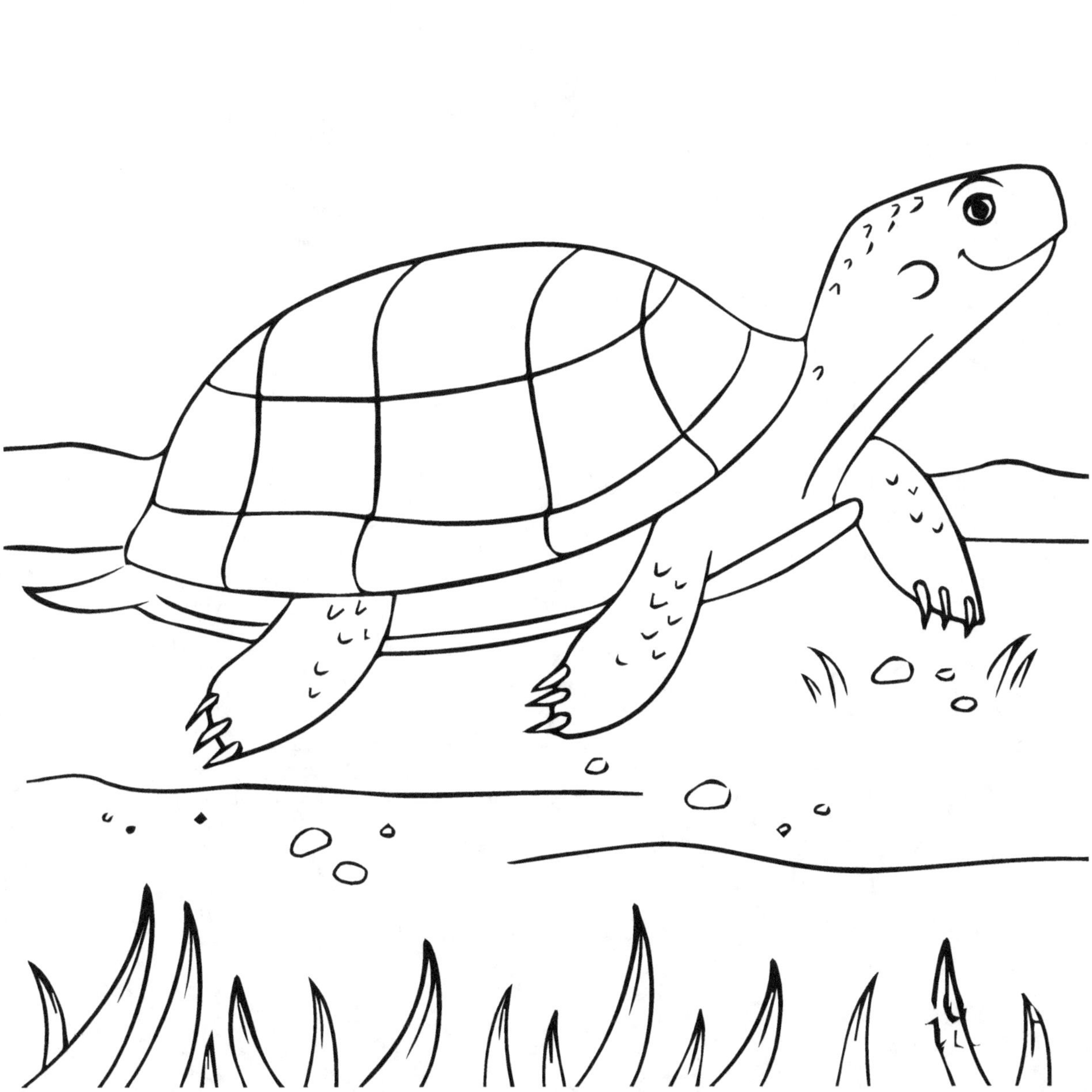

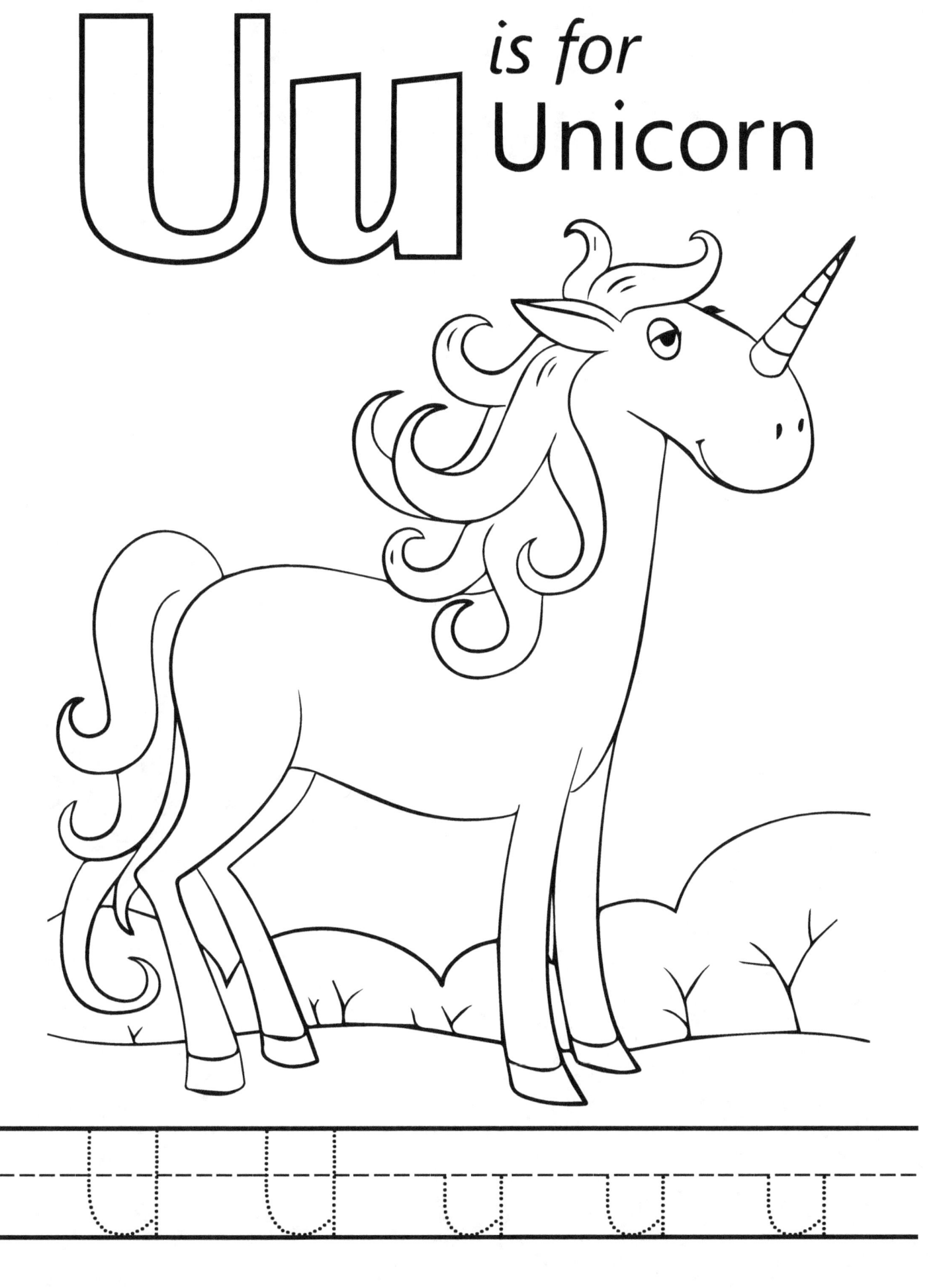

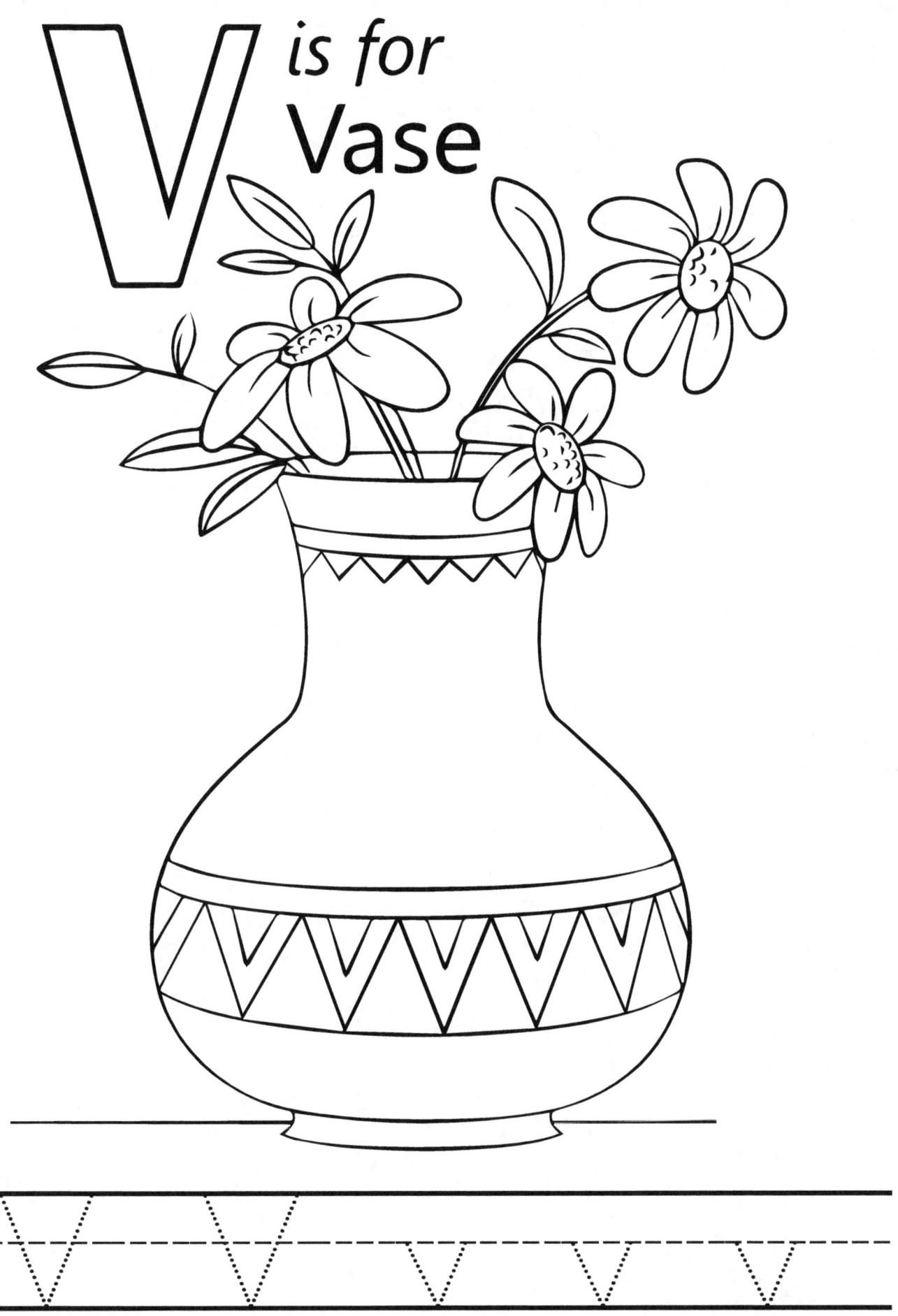

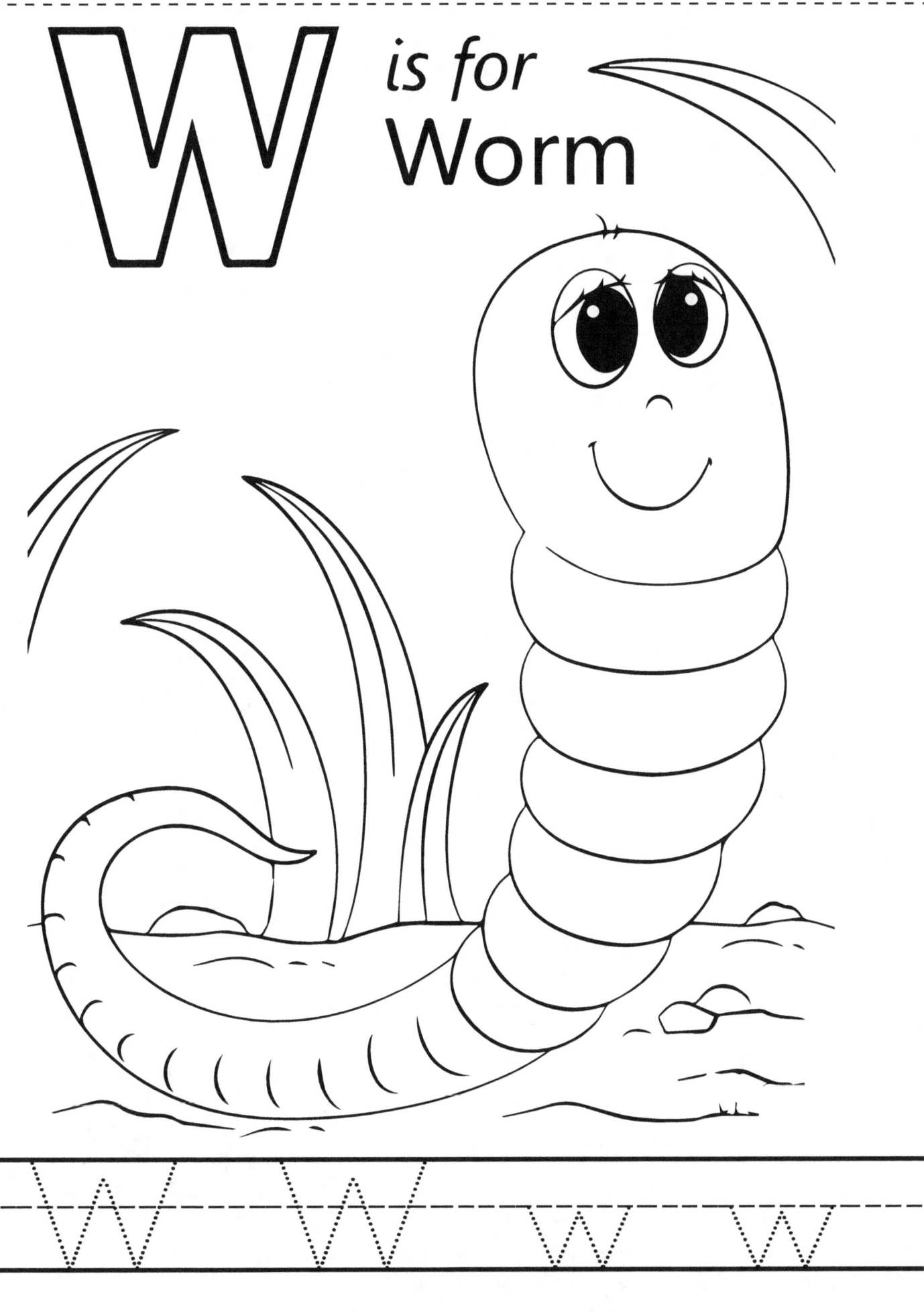

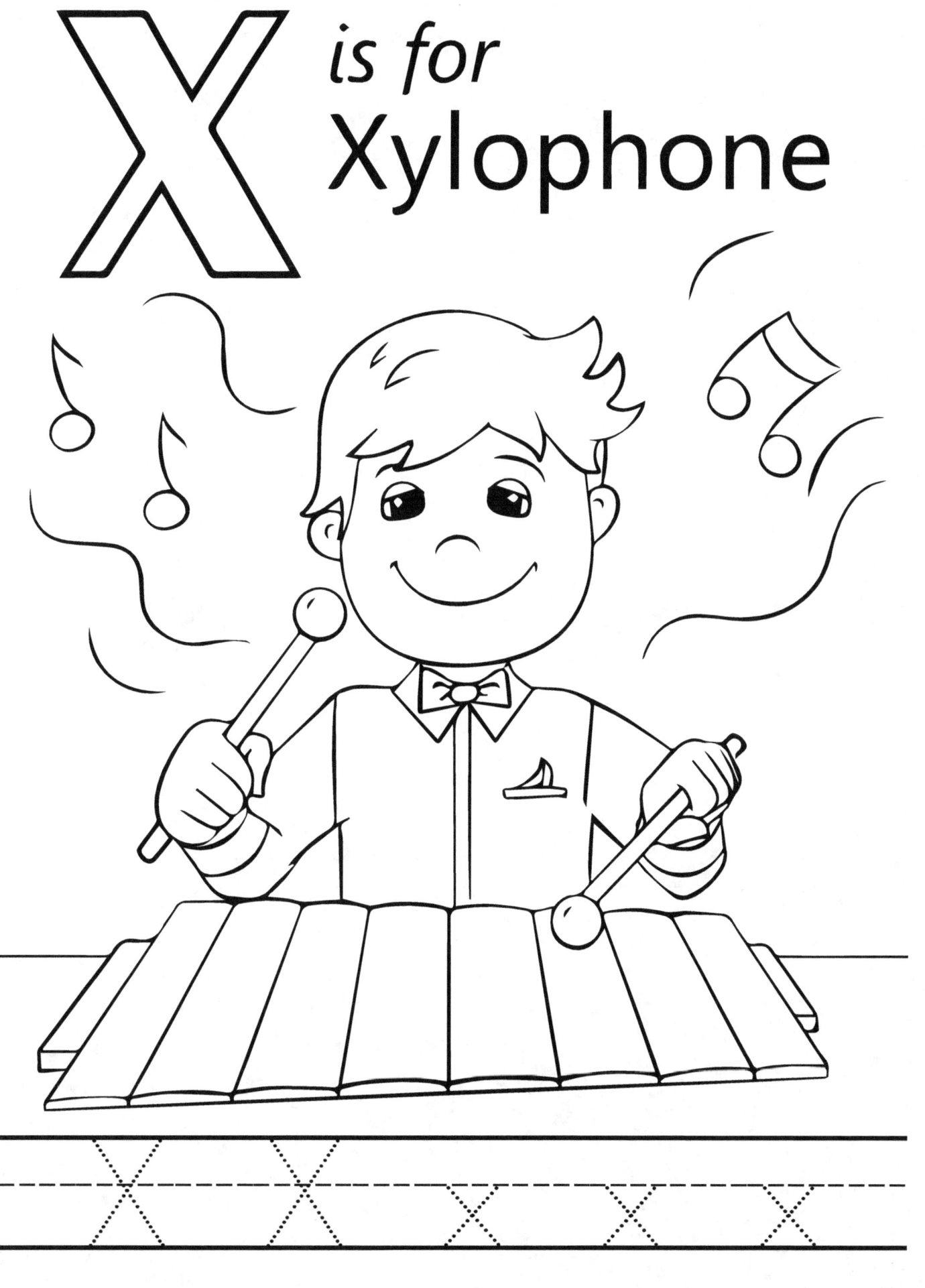

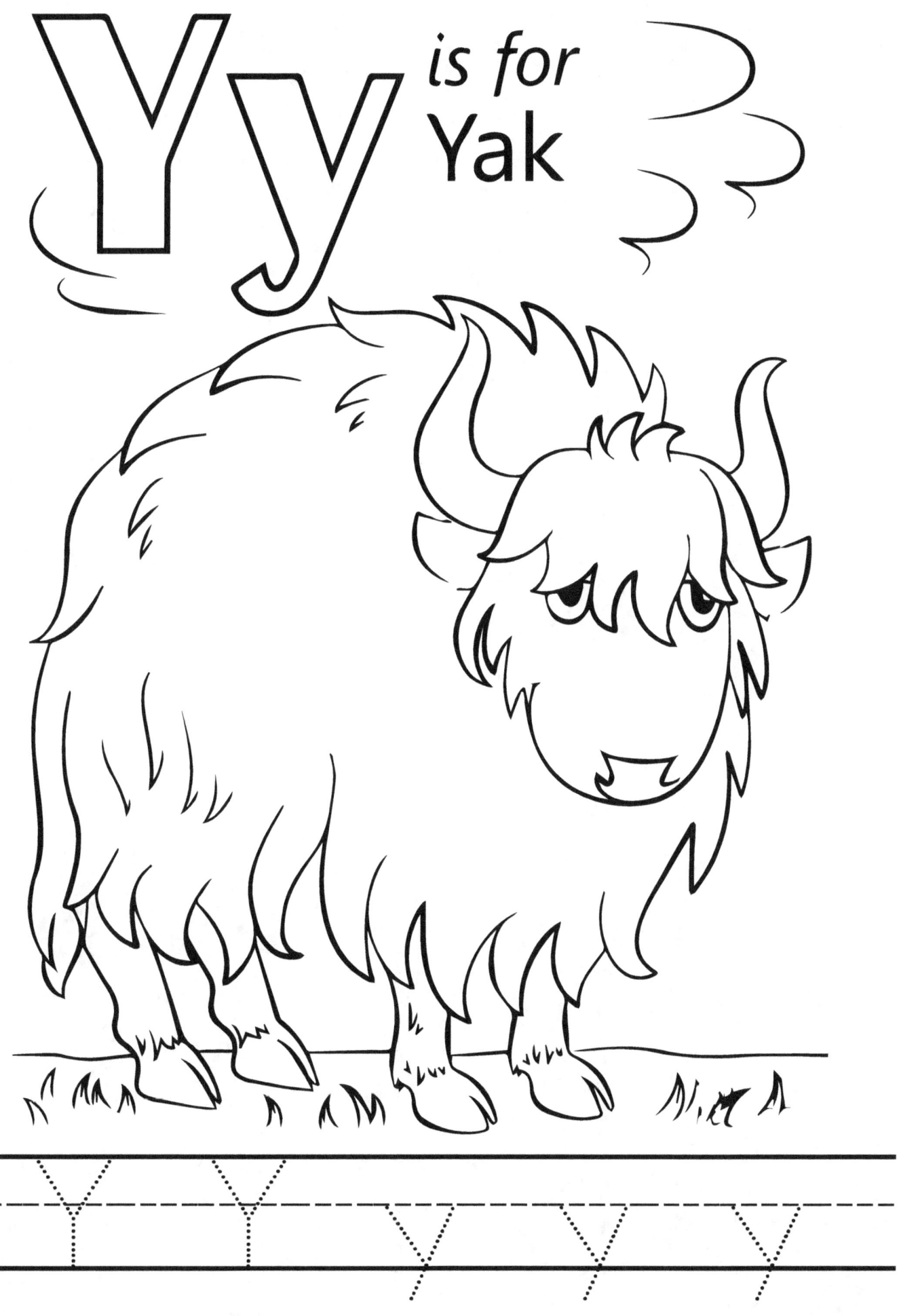

Z *is for* Zebra

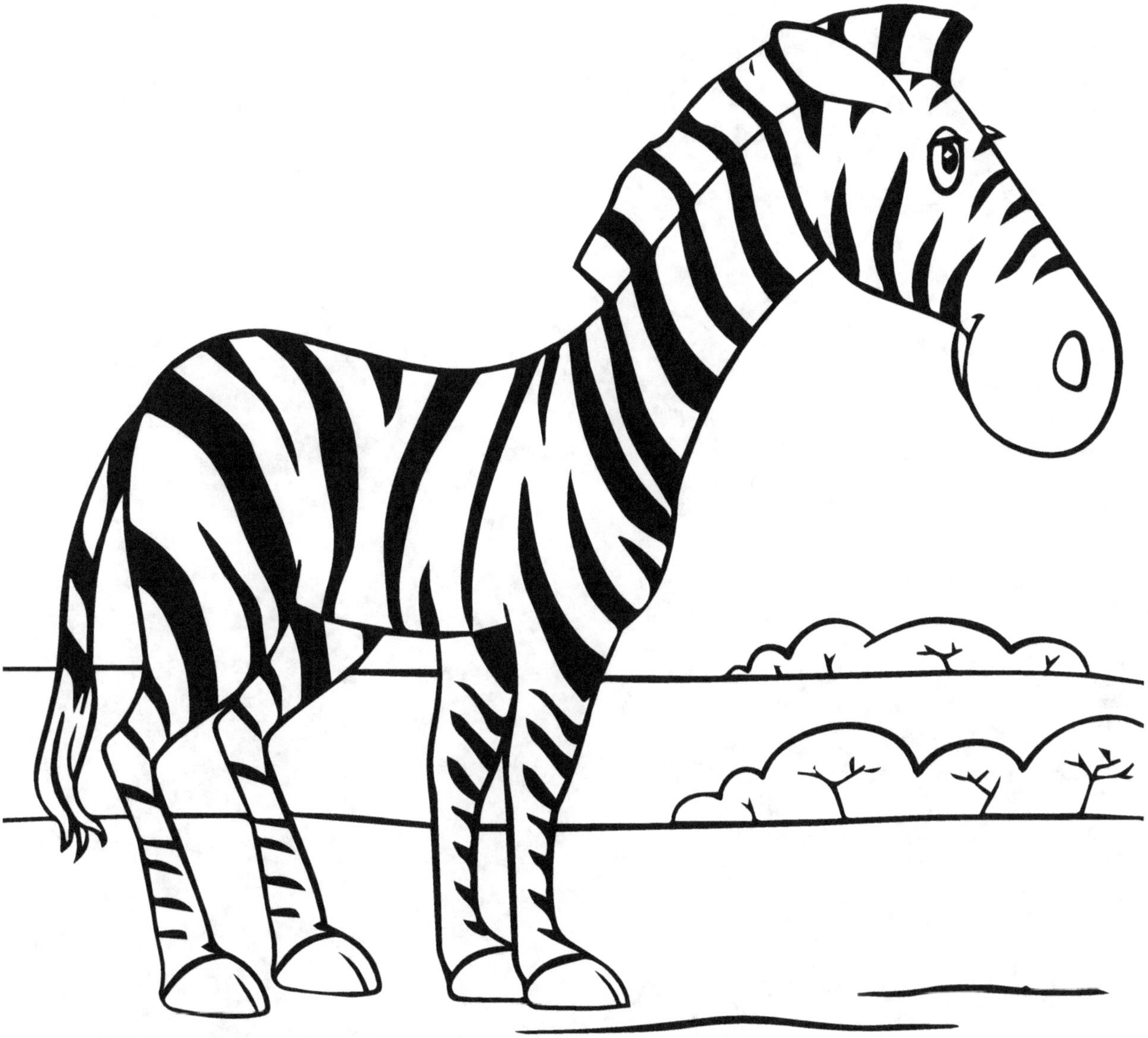

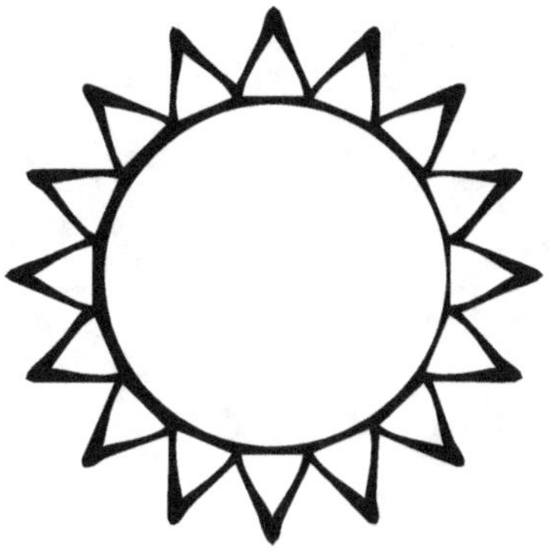

www.ingramcontent.com/pod-product-compliance
Lightning Source LLC
Chambersburg PA
CBHW080441220526
45465CB00007B/2725